THE DRAGON ON THE WALL

Also by Stanley Cook

The Squirrel In Town

STANLEY COOK
THE DRAGON ON THE WALL
and other poems

Illustrated by Liz Graham-Yooll

Blackie

To Kathleen

Acknowledgements are due to the BBC on whose Poetry Corner programme many of these poems have been broadcast.

Copyright © 1989 Stanley Cook
Illustrations © 1989 Liz Graham-Yooll
First published 1989 by Blackie and Son Ltd

All rights reserved. No part of this publication may be reproduced, stored in a retrieval system, or transmitted in any form or by any means, electronic, mechanical, photocopying, recording or otherwise without the written permission of the Publishers.

British Library Cataloguing in Publication Data

Cook, Stanley
 The dragon on the wall
 I. Title
 821'.914' 0809282

ISBN 0-216-92722-6

Blackie and Son Ltd
7 Leicester Place
London WC2H 7BP

Typeset by Jamesway Graphics
Middleton, Manchester M24 2HD

Printed in Great Britain

About the Author

Stanley Cook was born in Austerfield, South Yorkshire. He read English at Oxford and then taught in schools in Lancashire and Yorkshire. From 1969 to 1981 he lectured in English studies at Huddersfield Polytechnic. He has had several collections of adult poetry published, including *Form Photograph*, *Staff Photograph*, *Alphabet* and *Selected Poems* and he won first prize in the Cheltenham Festival Poetry Competition in 1972. His first collection for children was *The Squirrel In Town* published by Blackie, and he now regularly visits schools to work on poetry with children.

Introduction

A child's world is like any other we care to name—Shakespeare's or Lewis Carroll's, the scientific world or the business world—in being both limited but complete in all essentials for its independent existence. We can see that a child is limited but complete. The potential is there to deal with what lies outside the limitations. Television devotes much of its time to showing us people, animals and places of which we would otherwise have no knowledge. What it is doing in effect is showing how we would behave if we were Eskimos or lived in the Amazonian rain forest. Within the limitations of school, home and the neighbourhood, a child exercises the feelings and pursues the interests for which circumnavigating (or orbiting) the globe would give only more scope. For example, a swing, a slide or a climbing frame let the mind learn to conquer the air, the ocean and Everest. Even if the child does not go on to conquer Everest, the climbing frame has provided the authentic taste of a personal achievement.

It is like learning to read: acquiring the skill itself is *the* thing. If reading *Treasure Island* and *Gulliver's Travels* comes after that they will be no problem.

Life tends to become prose to adults, but to a young child it has the concentrated feeling of poetry. Young children's experiences at some point happen to them for the first time, however many times they may happen to them subsequently—however many times after the first time they have to be experienced before their full significance sinks in. There is, to take an obvious example, a first time when the seeds that went into the soil brown and dry emerge as fresh green shoots; water runs away and pins stick to the magnet for the first time. Such things are large as the landscape in which they occur: within a young child's mind such heroic figures as the school caretaker have the longest lease of credibility they could ever have. This is the time of life when everyone's mother lives in a big house and everyone's father has a big car. Shops and vehicles are as splendid as in later life they will only pretend to be, in the jargon of ad men. The small but intensely felt world is like one of those internally immense kingdoms that externally are the size of a raindrop in fairy tales. The child's world in some ways is less limited than our own, having room for a dragon to fly in at the window when ours has not.

A child's worldview is communicable to adults since they have corresponding feelings embedded at the back of their minds from their own childhood. In addition, when one takes a close look at a kite or a ball, they have very much to offer in their own right. They test the environment, swooping and hovering or bouncing and rolling to give expression to the forces that set the scene of our lives.

Similarly, a poem dips into the mind. It holds up and applauds, to the best of its literary ability, what the child has found: it gives a clap to lights for being bright and to lemonade for its tingle on the tongue. I hope that, from these poems, children and understanding adults will be able to relive times when they wondered at the snow in the playground, the lorry in the night and the dragon on the wall.

Stanley Cook

In the Playground

In the playground the railings are green,
Too narrow to put your head between
And there I skip like a bouncing ball
Or bounce my ball upon the wall.
When it rains the puddles are fun
To test the toes of my wellingtons.
When falling leaves come dodging down
We catch them before they reach the ground.
In Winter I glide
Along the slide
And snowballs make
My fingers ache.
In the playground
Some run round,
Some walk
And talk,
Some stand
On their hands
Against the wall
And some do nothing at all.

The Playground Gate

Both sides of the iron gate
The wall lines up
And the gate stands in the line
Whenever it is shut.

The gate and the wall
Have grown up tall and hard
And all round the playground
They stand on guard.

Cats still squeeze between
The iron bars of the gate
But when it is shut
People have to wait;

Until it is time
For the children to leave
And the gate swings slowly back
In one big farewell wave.

The Climbing Frame

The climbing frame is a tree of steel
Whose branches have no leaves
But stretch within my reach
And fit themselves beneath my feet.

Swiftly as a squirrel I climb
And through the branches I look down
At the faraway ground
Where everyone else is left behind.

High above the slide and swing
I perch like a bird in the top of a tree
And everyone stares up at me
When I begin to sing.

The Performing Bag

The plastic bag that once was full
Of coloured sweets was empty and lost
And lay against the playground wall,
Flat and still among the dust.

But a wind came up the road,
Brushing back the hair of the grass,
Trying to unbutton people's coats
And teasing the leaves as it passed.

It felt its way inside the bag
Like a hand inside a glove
And like a puppet waking up
The plastic bag began to move.

As the air inside it puffed it out,
The bag that was lying sad and flat
Began to waggle its corners about
And nodded its head this way and that.

It dodged its way between the children
Who watched it carried high in the sky
And disappear on the hand of the wind,
Waving them goodbye.

The Slide

Like the seagull I saw
Last summer at the seaside
Sitting on top of a wave
That washed it ashore,
On the playground slide
I come sweeping down;
And as for a moment I stand
At the bottom on dry land
Other children follow
Like more white waves
That break on the yellow sand.

The Swing

The swing is a seat on the air
That first of all moves as slow
As a wind beginning to blow
That gently brushes back my hair.

Then I stretch my legs out longer
As I make a bigger push
And higher and faster I rush
Like a wind that is getting stronger.

I drive the air on my narrow seat
While houses and trees flash by
And like the wind up in the sky
Push the clouds along with my feet.

The Dragon on the Wall

A bright green dragon comes in at the door
And crawls along the classroom wall.
He must be lost
Or need a rest
For he never came into the classroom before.

His body is hard as a fist with nobbly scales.
He could pull down a tree that he hooked with
    his tail.
He rests on the wall, his mouth open wide,
Puffing and panting flames from inside.

His green silky wings are raised on his back,
Ready to come down in one big flap
To carry him out of the open window
When no one's there to see him go.

When we leave him on his own
Does he fly home
In a streak of light
Through the black of the night
To see that his cave is safe
With all its bright shining gold?

Mr Fitzsimmons

Mr Fitzimmons
Our caretaker is tall
For reaching pictures
Down from the wall,
Looking over gates
And piled-up crates.
Just the height
To put new bulbs
In electric lights
Or discover
What was lost
On top of cupboards.
He has a key
Worn shiny in his pocket
For every door
And a polisher
Plugging in at the socket
For every floor,
He brushes school clean
And polishes it bright
Every night.

Growing Cress in a Polystyrene Trough

A polystyrene trough
Keeps seeds warm
And its thick white walls
Keep them from harm.

The cress seeds we planted
Were small as pencil dots
Spattering the soil
We put in the trough.

It took only two weeks
For them to grow
Into a thick green forest
In walls as white as snow.

Crayoning

The sheet of paper is white
And perfectly quiet
Like a drift of snow
Into which nobody goes
And out of which nothing shows.

Then I crayon a sun to shine
And the sky's blue line,
A red house with a green door
And a chimney above it all
Out of which the black smoke pours.

In the garden is a mother
Hanging out clothes of every colour;
And flowers of every colour grow
Where once the paper
Was white as snow.

Colouring

Fat coloured crayons,
Especially the red ones,
Rub their heads
Against the rough grey
Paper I draw on
On my table;
And thick black pencils
In wooden jackets
Rub their noses in books.
Paintbrushes dip
Their tongues in colours
And take long licks
At children's pictures
Pinned to easels;
And even my fingers
Want to put
Themselves in the paint
And make red marks
All over my work.

Why I Give People Green Hair

Did you ever hear
A hungry cow tear
Bunches of grass to eat
From the ground?
It makes a ripping sound
Like tearing a dress or trousers
And shuts the grass in the door of its teeth.

Grass is a beautiful colour.
No wonder cows like eating grass in Spring.
Next time I do a painting
I shall give myself and my mother
Hair of the brightest green
A cow has ever seen.

Paste

Paste needs stirring very well:
You stir a long time to make it thick
Like a witch who mixes a spell.
Paste is magic at sticking things together
And fixing pictures onto paper
As robbers in a story can't escape
When they're kept from moving by magic.
A wave of the brush and a touch of paste
Keeps everything in place.

Books

Books are sandwiches.
Between the front and back
Something good —
But not food —
Is tightly packed.
Stories and pictures
On slices of paper
That children sit
At their table to read
Bit by bit
Like mice at cheese.

Magnets

Magnets play catch
With bits of metal;
Magnets are made
With short thick arms
Like a letter u
And once one comes
Near tacks or nails
And drawing or safety pins
It's 'Got you!' —
They're fixed as firm
As if they were stuck with glue.
Magnets can find
Pins that hide
Among threads of cotton
Or on the other side
Of pieces of paper,
They pull tin lids
Across the floor,
And stick to the iron lock
On the door.
When a magnet plays catch
With the nails and pins,
It always wins.

Socks

Socks are so alike you can put
Either of them on either foot.

No use calling them names like Left and Right
For both of the pair are exactly alike.

Socks are twins who are always together
And never go anywhere without each other,

Together dry and together wet in the rain,
Together dirty and together clean;

You can't go out in one when the other is lost
At the back of a drawer or in the wash;

Together all day on your left leg and
   your right,
They're still together when you take them
   off at night.

To Make Jam Tarts

To make jam tarts we washed our hands
And put our caps and aprons on
(For when you're cooking you have to be clean)
And we thought how good our tarts would be.

We put two spoonfuls of flour each
And a piece this big of margarine
And so much sugar into a bowl
And we thought how good our tarts would be.

We added the water but not too much,
We used our hands to mix it all up
And it stuck to our fingers like crumbs of snow.
We kneaded and kneaded and kneaded it all,
Patting it to shape with our palms,
Till it made one big snowball
And we knew how good our tarts would be.

We rolled the dough with a rolling pin
And the lumps that wanted to be thick and fat
Had to lie down and be flat and thin
And we knew how good our tarts would be.

We cut out shapes with the cutter
And put the bright red jam on them
And dabs of pastry onto the jam.
We knew how good our tarts would be
And we greased the tins and put them in the
    oven.

While they cooked, we four washed up
And when the wonderful tarts were ready
We wrote a letter — 'Dear Mummy and
    Daddy,
Come and taste the tarts we have made' —
And of course they came, for they knew
How good our tarts would be.

Soap

Soap lives in water
And is hard to catch
Slipping through your fingers
Especially in the bath.

It hasn't a handle to hold
And can't be fastened with string;
It hasn't a zip to close
Or a cardboard box to go in.

It doesn't answer a whistle
Or come for milk or a biscuit;
It won't go into a kennel
Or curl up and sleep in a basket.

Soap is a square slippery fish:
I wish it would stay in its place
And not always vanish
While I'm washing my face.

Water

Water sits still in a bucket
Or a cup all day
Waiting for a chance
To run away.

Silently it squeezes
Its way outside
Through any crack
Or hole it can find.

It squeezes down
A plastic funnel,
Crowding into
A plastic bottle.

From a big beaker
It will go
Into a little one
Until it overflows.

Water likes best
To be running free
Down a river
Into the sea.

Dressing Up

I sometimes think that you are a prince,
I am really a princess
And people would know I was
If I wore the right kind of dress.

I haven't a crown but I put a hat
With a long feather on my head;
The sleeves of my dress shine like the sun
With all their glittering golden thread.

The sequins twinkle like the stars,
Scattered all over it,
And when I am bigger my silver shoes
Will be a perfect fit.

I really am a princess
And when I'm dressed up you can see
I'm not an ordinary girl
But only pretending to be.

The Room

A cardboard box is a room
Whose roof is a lid
Where anyone wanting a home
Can come to live.

Bend a flap of cardboard back
To make a door
And use a folded handkerchief
To carpet the floor.

Cover the brown cardboard walls
With flowery paper
And put in a table and chairs
And a bed and a cooker.

It's too small and I'm too big
For me to get inside
But here's a doll without a home,
Just the right size.

The Perfect Meal

Over the crisp fish fingers
Steams of tomato ketchup spread,
Colouring them and the chips
A beautiful red.

I wave the bottle like a wand
Over every finger and chip,
Making them lovely to see and eat
With magic blobs of it.

Tomato ketchup works wonders
For the food it falls upon;
I shake the turned-up bottle
Till all the magic is gone.

Chips

Out of the paper bag
Comes the hot breath of the chips
And I shall blow on them
To stop them burning my lips.

Before I leave the counter
The woman shakes
Raindrops of vinegar on them
And salty snowflakes.

Outside the frosty pavements
Are slippery as a slide
But the chips and I
Are warm inside.

A Gingerbread House

Some houses are made to live in
With bedrooms, a lounge and a kitchen:
The walls are so strong and thick
The cat can't scratch a hole with its paws
And has to come in at the door
And the sun can't melt the brick.

But as a special treat
Some houses are made to eat:
You put the chimney in your mouth
Or a chocolate door or window;
You eat the walls and roof
And afterwards tell everybody
One day you were so hungry
You ate a house.

The Lolly

Inside the fridge is frost
On the ice cream blocks
As if the winter were locked
Inside a box.

Outside the pavements burn
Beneath my feet.
I feel myself melt
In drops of sweat with the heat.

The woman gives me
A piece of ice on a stick,
From the orange juice sea
A frozen wave to lick.

Ice-Cream and Fizzy Lemonade

Ice-cream is sliding, soft and cold
And gives a smooth and soothing coat
On hot summer days
To the back of your throat.

Fizzy lemonade looks like water
But as you unscrew the bottle top
Bubbles crowd together in froth
With a rushing sound and a sudden pop.

It prickles and tickles your nose
And tingles the back of your throat
That needs another sliding soft ice-cream
To give it back a smooth and soothing coat.

Ice-Cream Vans

Ice-cream vans are the prettiest to see
Of all the shops on wheels in the road.
They are coloured as creamy white
As their own ice-cream and ribboned with gold.

I like to hear them play their tunes
Like a travelling musical box.
I like to lay my tongue against
Their cold, sweet lollipops.

Teaching A Ball

Whether it is large or small
It seems that a ball
Can never know
Which way to go.

To find its way round
The park and playground
You have to help it
By giving it a kick,

By rolling it here and there,
By throwing it into the air
And catching it as it falls,
And bouncing it on the walls.

Every day
You take it out to play
Until there's nothing it hasn't seen
And nowhere it hasn't been.

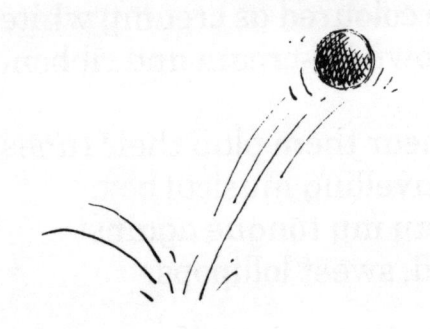

Skittles

The skittles stand with hands in pockets
Of their long brown jackets
And though they're tall
The fat little wooden ball
Hits them with a smack
And tumbles two on their backs
Where rolling rumbling round
They knock the others down
And all fall flat.

It was done only in fun
And the wooden men
Get up on their feet again
Still with their hands in the pockets
Of their long brown jackets.

Finding a Slide

The playground is covered with snow today
And in the snow is hidden away
A new, exciting game
For you to play.

Hidden beneath the snow is a slide
That you use your feet to find,
Pushing the snow onto one side
To find a path of shining ice
That was waiting all the time
To give you a ride.

Along you glide
And sometimes fall down flat
And slide along on your back,
But however you go
You give an extra shine
To the game you found in the snow.

The Kite

On a windy day
When hats and newspaper
Go blowing by
And even the leaves
Are torn away,
The kite spreads its arms out wide,
Hops and steps along the ground
And with the help of the wind
Learns to fly.

It rises high in the sky
At the end of its long line,
Ties itself to the top
Of the tallest tree
And never again comes down.

The Coming of the Snowmen

Strange things begin to happen
When everywhere is hidden
Under a sudden fall of snow
And the winter winds blow.

In the house frost flowers cover
The inside of windows all over,
Ice on their pond keeps ducks from diving in
And they skid and slip where they used to swim.

In this, their favourite weather, the snowmen come
From the frozen lands the winds blow from,
Big, strange men whose heads are completely round,
Standing in the garden, street or playground.

You always find them standing on their own
As if they don't mind being alone;
However cold it becomes, they never care
And ask for nothing but an old hat to wear.

They haven't come to snowball or slide
But just to enjoy the snow and ice;
As long as they last, the snowmen stay
And when they go the snowmen, too, melt away.

David and Goliath

Goliath the Giant
Crushed the grass
Like an elephant
In walking past.

Like passengers
Upstairs on the bus
Or a man on a ladder
He could look down on us.

Birds sometimes mistook
Him for a tree
But David was small
As you and me.

David's friends
Were in terrible trouble
Until he felled
Goliath with a pebble.

Like a works chimney
He fell to the ground
Or a useless building
That men knock down.

He lay in a heap
And the ground shook
Like a load tipped
From a tipping truck.

David was brave
Although he was small
And fought for his friends
And saved them all.

If Someone Small Lived on the Floor

If someone small
Lived on the floor
All he could see
In the classroom would be
The ends of table legs
Like tiptoes of trees
With the rest far above his head.
Coloured monsters
In plastic and leather
Shiny skins
Would trample up to him
And block out the view
And how would he know
It was only you
In your shoes?

Flowering Umbrellas

Umbrellas are folded up like buds.
But umbrella buds don't open in the sun.
They flower in the rain instead
In all kinds of colours: black, green and red,
Brown and white, and checked and striped.
Outside the school in the rain mothers stand
With umbrella flowers growing from their
   hands.

Trains

The doors shut, the horn sounds,
The driving wheels begin to turn:
All kinds of trains begin to run
On railways all over the world.

Trains are running past the tigers
Sheltering from the sun
And past the elephants in the river
Cooling themselves in the mud.

Trains you see on television
Or hear about at story time
Hoot a hippopotamus
Away from the line.

Trains are passing signals
When the light is green
And people on trains are waving
To people in the fields.

Trains that have come a long way
And still have a long way to go
Are racing along the rails
Of their iron road.

The driver sits in his cabin,
As I do in mine,
Driving past people, tigers, elephants
And a hippopotamus beside the line.

The Bus

Beneath its cover
The engine turns over
Sounding loud and hot
As it waits at the stop,
Thudding like feet
Or a drum-beat.
People push
Onto the bus:
Women in hats,
Men in caps,
Boys in shirts
And girls in skirts
With hair cut long;
Mothers help
Small children on.
With thank you's and please's
The conductor squeezes
To take the fares.
'One and two halves
'And one for him downstairs.'
'Into town'
And 'all the way'.
'I've lost my purse
And I can't pay'.
'I've dropped my money
Under the seat.

See if it's rolled
Beneath your feet'.
'One for me
And one for the dog'.
In the sun, rain,
Snow and fog,
In the day
And in the dark,
Past people at windows
And trees in the park,
No time to stop
For sweets in shops,
Picking up
And putting down,
The double-decker
Goes into town.

The Lamp Birds

Day is over and under bridges
And blades of grass, in shady corners
And empty rooms and down deep holes
And up the chimneys darkness gathers.

One crossing beacon winks at the other
And orange lamps light up in the street;
The lamp posts bend as if a bird
Were perching there, holding the light in its
    beak.

All over town like tall stone trees
The lamp posts stand in the night,
A stone bird perched on every one
Holding up its orange light.

On a String

As I walk along the pavement
The houses and people stare
To see me trailing a piece of string
Behind me everywhere.

It's frayed at the end
From being dragged along
And dirty from going in puddles
And being trodden on.

But at the end I shall see
One day when I look back
A curly-haired dog behind me
With its white coat patched with black.

The Pavement

Pavements are made
Of squares of stone
To play a long game
Of hopscotch on.

Into the distance
They stretch away
In a game of hopscotch
Too long to play.

Round the houses
And back again
Is marked for a game
That never ends.

Tulips on the Roundabout

The tulips stand where nobody goes
On the roundabout between the roads,
Some with yellow turbans on their heads
And some with red.
One road goes to the works
And one to school,
One under the railway bridge
And one to the swimming pool.

Peeping and screeching, the cars go past
The tulips in their turbans on the grass
That never seem to notice
The lorries rumbling round
But stand quite still
On their special piece of ground,
As if they had flown through the air
On a green magic carpet
And landed there.

In the Street

The fat old pillar-box in the street
Has a red and black jersey down to its feet
And keeps its big mouth open wide
To take the letters into its inside.

In the evening in the cold and damp
On one long leg stands the new street lamp.
High above us in its beak it holds
A golden fish it caught in the road.

The light at the crossing goes in and out
As if someone were blowing up
And letting down a round balloon
Or switching on and off the moon.

Zebra Crossing

Along the rows of houses
Run roads that run into roads
Carrying cars full of people
And lorries with heavy loads
Taking turns to go
As if in a game they play
That keeps them occupied
The whole of every day.
Straight past the post office
And round the corner shop
The traffic on the road
Plays its game non-stop.

But at the black and white
  stripes,
The zigzag lines
And shining giant oranges
Of the zebra crossing signs
I hold my mother's hand
Standing waiting to see
The lorries, cars and buses
Stop and wait for me.

Clocks

White-faced clocks are sitting or standing
Spending every minute of their lives
Trying to see that everything
Happens exactly on time.

When you listen to the clock
You can hear how it counts
How much longer it is
To the time someone wants.

Like children counting on fingers
Clocks count on pointed wheels
That tick, as they turn inside them,
The times that people need.

Small clocks on fireplaces
Have only one room to look round
But big clocks on towers
Watch the whole town.

Clocks don't say
A word to anyone
But point with their hands
When the time has come:

Time for shops to raise their blinds
Like an eyelid from an eye,
Time for buses to travel the road to town
And time for the brightly polished sun
To start its journey across the sky.

Time to get dressed and have breakfast
And time for fathers to go to work,
Time to put the letters through the box
And the milk on the step.

Time to brush your hair and teeth,
Time to walk to school
Past the clock looking down
And pointing to twenty to nine
High above the streets.

The Bread Shop

I know they sell bread at the bread shop,
Big and small loaves with crusts as brown
As the ears of corn were in the fields
Before the farmer cut them down.

And men who are mending the road outside
Who stop for a drink and something to eat
Tramp into the bread shop for sandwiches
Folding breadcakes round slices of meat.

But have you seen the trays of tarts
With shores of pastry round red jam lakes
Or the line of jam and line of cream
Drawn side by side in the yellow cake?

More than five and more than ten
Iced buns with cherries dropped
Bright red and glistening
Into the snowdrift of icing on top.

More eclairs, those pods of chocolate
Bursting open with fillings of cream,
And brandy snaps, those crispy tunnels,
Than at any party where I've been.

We buy the biscuits, we buy the bread,
Sugar, sauce and cornflakes
And then my mother says
'You choose the cakes.'

The Fire Station

As I went by
The tall thin tower
Where the hoses
Hang to dry
And the big glass doors
With fire engines
Redder than fire
Lined up inside,
A bell began to ring,
Fluttering its metal tongue
Against its metal lips,
And men from upstairs
Slid down a pole
And hurried on
Coats and helmets.
The fire engine started,
The doors were opened wide
And a man went into the road
To stop the cars.
Sirens were panting out
A frightened sound
And flashing blue lights
Were spinning round.
People came out of shops
To stand and stare
And buses pulled
Into the side.

A house, a chip pan,
A works or a chimney
Burnt somewhere.
The bright red engine
With its crew
Raced to the rescue.

The Doctor's Waiting Room

The doctor's waiting room
Is the place where people come
To talk to the receptionist
Or read all kinds of notices
With letters in big black print
And magazines and comics
Or listen to telephones ring
Or play with the building bricks
Out of a plastic bucket
Or sit very still
And stay very quiet.

By the time they call your name
To go tell the doctor
What's the matter
You've almost forgotten the ache or pain
Because of which you came.

The Face of the House

The sun wakes up the house
And the windows open their eyes,
Blinking back their curtains
To watch the bright sun rise.

The face of the house is flat and square
And from beside the mouth of the door
The eyes of two windows stare
And under the hat of the roof two more.

All day long
The houses sit
Staring into the eyes
Of houses opposite.

But when night pulls its blanket
Of darkness over the street
The window curtains close like eyelids
And the houses fall asleep.

The New Coat

The house had a coat
That was getting old,
Thin all over
And sometimes in holes.

Painters in white overalls
Came one summer day
And scraped and burnt
The old coat of paint away.

They gave our house
The brightest coat in the row
While they sang and whistled
And played their radio.

What colour is the coat?
If you want to know that
Look at my hands
And the tail of our cat.

How to Build a House

To build a house you need a painted hut
You bring to the site on the back of a lorry
And other men to help you put it up.

To build a house you need to drink your tea
In the painted hut when a whistle blows
And twiddle your mug to empty the leaves.

To build a house you need to dirty your clothes,
Wear a yellow helmet or a big-peaked cap
And use a coloured handkerchief to blow your
    nose.

To build a house when the weather is hot
You need a check shirt to take off
And a belt with a buckle round your
    trouser-top.

To build a house you need to be strong enough
To dig foundations out to start the wall
And climb a ladder after it as it rises up.

To build a house you need to know all
The people who pass and shout to them
    'Hello, Jack!'
And 'Hello' to me, although I'm still small.

Red

Red is loud and shouts,
The colour of fire engines
And the topmost traffic light.
Red asks people to notice
Cones round holes in the road;
Red cherries and strawberries
And hips and haws
Ask for notice
From the birds.
When I'm painting,
Red is the colour I like best
And use more often than the rest.

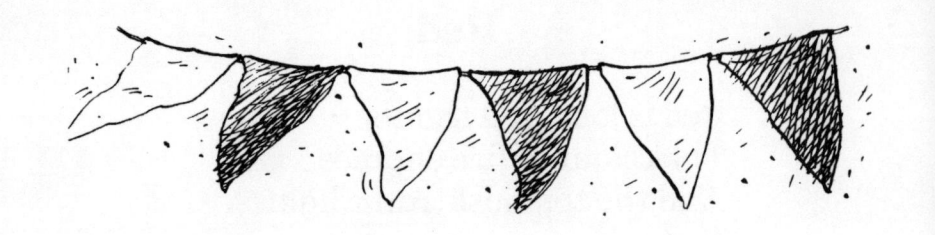

The Parade

Drums beat,
Bugles blow,
Sirens sound,
Balloons
Burst with a bang,
Bells ring,
Pipes play,
People sing.

All the traffic stops
Or has to go a different way
And people line the road
On the day of the big parade.

Men march,
Girls dance,
All the vans,
Carts and lorries
Are in fancy dress.

I sit on my father's shoulders
So I can see.
I wave to the parade
And from the lorries
That look like castles,
Space ships,
Monsters,
Houses,
Or desert islands,
Everyone waves back at me.

Going to the Launderette

When my mother goes
To the launderette down the road
She packs a case with clothes
As if we were going away
For an hour's holiday.

While the clothes are washing clean
Twisting like snakes in the machine
She sits with her friends on the row of seats
Or helps them stretch and fold their sheets.

I watch through the glass of the drier door
The cloth snakes climb up the curving wall
Until it stops and back they fall
Tired with trying to its floor.

Stamps

With every letter
You send a picture,
The stamp you lick
And stick on the envelope,
Often of famous people
But often as well
Pictures pretty enough to put
Into a book —

Aeroplanes, trains and cars,
Birds and beautiful flowers,
Butterflies, bridges,
Castles, churches
And at Christmas
The shepherds, kings and angels
You sing of in carols.

But I haven't noticed yet
Any pictures of pirates
Or pets I have kept
Or flowers I have grown:
I shall get my pencils out
And make some stamps of my own.

Letters

Letters are pushed through the flap,
Dive through the air and flop on the mat,
Or sulk inside the letter box,
Annoyed at being trapped;
Or in the morning the postman knocks
And hands your letters in
Before they get up to anything;

Or pushes them under the door
And sends them skidding across the floor.
Letters let people send
Good news and wishes to their friends.
Letters come in trains,
Ships and aeroplanes
From islands in the sea
Where monkeys use the trees
For climbing-frames.
Letters come from aunts
With birthday presents;
From a stamp the Queen in her crown
In a brown or green picture looks down
On your name and address that they wrote
In the middle of the envelope.
Letters come to school
From people who are ill
Saying 'Thank you, children,
For the messages and lovely flowers'.
Letters ask you away
For a fortnight's holiday
With your grandpa and grandmother
When the sun is an oven in summer
Baking your arms and legs
And the bald top
Of grandpa's head
As brown as a crust of bread.
Letters have to be carried,
But they wish they could walk;
And letters have to be read,
But they wish they could talk.

Cutting the Hedge

Two or three times a year
My father trims
The hedge of our garden
With hungry snapping shears.

Their long mouth opens wide,
Takes a bite
At pieces of privet
And tosses them aside.

The privet reaches so high
My father stands
On a step ladder
To cut it out of the sky.

I am standing there
Below the ladder
And small leaves flutter
Down and into my hair.

Like big green raindrops
They go down the back of my neck
And I stand beneath the shower
Without ever getting wet.

The Lorry in the Night

Out of the works comes the lorry
With four bright headlamps like glaring eyes
In the head of a huge monster
To let it see its way in the dark.

Like a monster making its way
Into the dark depths of a cave
It growls along past our house and its lights,
Carrying its load into the night.

As I watch from my window,
Into the night it burrows,
Shaking houses at the roadside,
The engine grumbling in its inside.

All night it will roar along the road
Till the sun rises for another day
And at another works far away
The lorry will deliver its heavy load.

Television Aerials

Television aerials
Look like witches' brooms.
When they finish flying
They leave them on the roof.

Television aerials
Are sticks to prod the sky
To make clouds full of rain
Hurry by.

Television aerials
Reach above chimney tops
To make a perch
Where tired birds can stop.

Television aerials
Are fixed to the chimney side
To rake us songs and pictures
Out of the sky.

A Bridge

A bridge is a giant on hands and knees
Kneeling down to fill a gap
And let people cross it on his back.

A bridge is a giant of stone or steel
With a back so hard he doesn't feel
The prodding of sticks or hammering of heels.

A bridge is a giant who carries the road
And the lorries on it with heavy loads,
A giant who stays there night and day
And never gets up and goes away.

The Bulldozer

An orange-coated man
Who wears for his work
The colour of coat
You see in the dark
Starts the engine
Bang-b-bang-bang.

The bulldozer scoop
Is like a big boot
As if a giant
Smoothed the ground
With the side of his foot
Down-d-down-down.

Digging its tracks
Into the mud
The yellow bulldozer
Bends it back
Like a butting bull
Charge-ch-charge-thud.

It lifts loose earth
Away from its feet
And drops it in a heap
Or dumps it in a truck
Bump-b-bump-full.

The Dustman

If it weren't for the dustman
Who comes to take our rubbish away
There'd soon be no room in the house
For us to eat or sleep or play.

Instead of us, piles of papers
Would sit on all the chairs
And plastic wrapping and cardboard boxes
Would keep us from going upstairs.

In the kitchen corner would stand
Empty box on empty box
Reaching right to the ceiling
Like a tower of building blocks.

Watch me to see how to put
Rubbish nobody needs in a sack;
Watch me to see how the dustman
Takes the sack away on his back.

A Knee Is a Chair to Sit On

A knee is a chair to sit on
When you are tired,
Sometimes hard and strong
Like chairs in a classroom,
Sometimes soft as a cushion
And soft enough to sleep on
At the fireside.

Too Tired

The tortoise that rang a bell
Somewhere inside its shell
As you pulled it along
And the lamb that turned
Its head from side to side
Stand in the back of a truck
As if they were tired of walking
And waited for a ride.

The dolls have stopped talking
And close their eyes in a cot,
The Teddy Bear lies sprawled out
With his ribbon untied
In the corner of a box.

The ducks are out of the water
And perch on the window ledge;
Among the books on the shelf
The rabbit is wedged
In a burrow all to himself.

Time to draw the curtains
And close the dolls' house door;
I and the toys are too tired
To play a minute more.

Index of First Lines

A bridge is a giant on hands and knees	73
A bright green dragon comes in at the door	15
A cardboard box is a room	29
A knee is a chair to sit on	76
A polystyrene trough	17
Along the rows of houses	53
An orange-coated man	74
As I walk along the pavement	49
As I went by	58
Beneath its cover	46
Books are sandwiches	21
Both sides of the iron gate	10
Day is over and under bridges	48
Did you ever hear	20
Drums beat,	64
Fat coloured crayons,	19
Goliath the Giant	42
I know they sell bread at the bread shop	56
I sometimes think that you are a prince,	28
Ice cream is sliding, soft and cold	34
Ice cream vans are the prettiest to see	35
If it weren't for the dustman	75
If someone small	43
In the playground the railings are green	9
Inside the fridge is frost	33
Letters are pushed through the flap,	68
Like the seagull I saw	13
Magnets play catch	22
Mr Fitzsimmons	16
On a windy day	39
Out of the paper bag	31
Out of the works comes the lorry	71

The ducks are out of the water
And perch on the window ledge;
Among the books on the shelf
The rabbit is wedged
In a burrow all to himself.

Time to draw the curtains
And close the dolls' house door;
I and the toys are too tired
To play a minute more.

Index of First Lines

A bridge is a giant on hands and knees	73
A bright green dragon comes in at the door	15
A cardboard box is a room	29
A knee is a chair to sit on	76
A polystyrene trough	17
Along the rows of houses	53
An orange-coated man	74
As I walk along the pavement	49
As I went by	58
Beneath its cover	46
Books are sandwiches	21
Both sides of the iron gate	10
Day is over and under bridges	48
Did you ever hear	20
Drums beat,	64
Fat coloured crayons,	19
Goliath the Giant	42
I know they sell bread at the bread shop	56
I sometimes think that you are a prince,	28
Ice cream is sliding, soft and cold	34
Ice cream vans are the prettiest to see	35
If it weren't for the dustman	75
If someone small	43
In the playground the railings are green	9
Inside the fridge is frost	33
Letters are pushed through the flap,	68
Like the seagull I saw	13
Magnets play catch	22
Mr Fitzsimmons	16
On a windy day	39
Out of the paper bag	31
Out of the works comes the lorry	71

Over the crisp fish fingers	30
Paste needs stirring very well:	21
Pavements are made	50
Red is loud and shouts,	63
Soap lives in water	26
Socks are so alike you can put	23
Some houses are made to live in	32
Strange things begin to happen	40
Television aerials	72
The climbing frame is a tree of steel	11
The doctor's waiting room	59
The doors shut, the horn sounds	45
The fat old pillar-box in the street	52
The house had a coat	61
The plastic bag that once was full	12
The playground is covered with snow today	38
The sheet of paper is white	18
The skittles stand with hands in pockets	37
The sun wakes up the house	60
The swing is a seat on the air	14
The tortoise that rang a bell	76
The tulips stand where nobody goes	50
To build a house you need a painted hut	62
To make jam tarts we washed our hands	24
Two or three times a year	70
Umbrellas are folded up like buds	44
Water sits still in a bucket	27
When my mother goes	66
Whether it is large or small	36
White-faced clocks are sitting or standing	54
With every letter	66